CW01084941

First published 1999
Text and illustrations © Glennie Kindred 1999

Published by Wooden Books Ltd.
Walkmill, Cascob, Presteigne, Powys, Wales LD8 2NT

British Library Cataloguing in Publication Data
Kindred, G.
A Hedgerow Cookbook

A CIP catalogue record for this book is
available from the British Library

ISBN 1 902418 11 5

Printed and bound in Great Britain
by the Cromwell Press,
Trowbridge, Wiltshire

A
HEDGEROW
COOKBOOK

written and illustrated by

Glennie Kindred

This book is dedicated to Mother Earth in gratitude for all her abundant gifts, and to my children, Jerry, Jack and May

My heartfelt thanks to sister Suz for her help and friendship, and to my partner Brian Boothby for his love and appreciation. Also many thanks to John Martineau for providing the opportunity for me to share my knowledge and my art.

My favourite Herbal is "A Moden Herbal" by Mrs. M. Grieve; A good Field Guide is "Wild Flowers of Britain" by Roger Phillips.

CONTENTS

INTRODUCTION

Hedgerow cookery is an experience, an experiment, and a delight for all those interested in our native plants, our history, herbal medicines, and above all, food.

I use 'hedgerow' as a loose term, to include plants found in meadows and woodlands, and garden escapes which may be found wherever humans have inhabited in the past or present.

If you have a garden, let a bit of the wilderness in, and put aside an area where edible wild plants can grow. Many of these will thrive in shaded areas and in poor soils, along the hedgerows of your garden, and can be harvested as and when needed. No garden is without weeds, but if you eat them as well, then 'weeding' becomes 'harvesting'. I have also included some garden plants which are worth growing for their food value.

Knowing which plants are edible, where to find them and when to find them, brings a deeper connection to our natural world, and brings you full circle to the knowledge of our ancestors.

Brassington 1999

HEDGEROW COOKERY

Hedgerow cookery is not a survival test (although your knowledge may prove useful to you one day). There is no need for the whole meal to come from the wild. Use it more as an exciting addition to your usual food. I have only made suggestions for vegetarian food in this book, but meat and fish can of course be added to many of the recipes. The most important thing is a willingness to try new tastes and experiment. Use the basic recipes and add your own interpretations and flair.

The book has four sections: Spring, Summer, Autumn and Winter, with plants and recipes for each season. There are always overlaps either side of each season, so check ahead. It is essential to use a good field guide. Don't worry, your confidence will grow rapidly from one year to the next. I have purposefully chosen common plants, which are easy to identify, and safe to use.

With so many plants to choose from, and the ever changing seasonal varieties, hedgerow cookery opens many doors for a varied and interesting source of free food.

FORAGING TIPS

Buy a good field guide. I have purposefully chosen only plants which are common, easy to recognise and which cannot be confused with anything poisonous, but it is still important to make sure you are picking the right thing.

Gather on a dry day only where you are allowed and away from fields which may have been sprayed with chemicals.

Handle the plants as little as possible, putting them in paper bags or a wicker basket. Eat as soon as you can.

Only pick where there is a great profusion of the plant. Do not over-pick, especially from one plant. Use a pair of secateurs or scissors.

Build up a wild food map of your area, so that the next year you can return to rediscover the things you liked.

Investigate friends' gardens, plant shops and garden centres for edible wild flowers and herbs which you could plant along your own garden hedgerows - for easy foraging

SPRING

green vegetables, stems & salad plants

Wild greens are at their best in March, April and May, when the young leaves are sweet and tender. These plants have been eaten since the earliest times - it is only in the last hundred years or so so that we have narrowed our tastes solely down to cultivated vegetables. In many other countries, however, people still gather food from the wild.

Many of these plants are powerful spring tonics and will give a good boost to the system, especially when eaten in salad. Include a variety of these 'pot-herbs' for a spinach-type mixture, or add them to soups and stews. A list of spring plants begins below and continues overleaf.

Alexanders (*smyrnium olusatrum*). The leaves can be used in white sauce, in soups, or battered and deep-fried. The stems can be steamed and eaten like asparagus. The roots are like parsnip and the flower-buds can be used in a salad.

Bistort (*polygonum bistorta*). A spring tonic herb, traditionally used in the making of herb puddings. Use like spinach and also in soups.

SPRING

burdock, chickweed, comfrey & dandelion

Burdock (lesser) (arctium minus). Only the youngest leaves are to be eaten as spinach or in salads. The stems can be stripped and eaten in salads or steamed like asparagus. One of the best blood purifiers and tonics.

Chickweed (stellaria media). Cook the whole plant as a spinach vegetable and add to soups. Add the young leaves to salad. Traditionally eaten to build up the blood and strengthen the heart.

Comfrey (symphytum officinale). Long used as a vegetable in Ireland. Add the young leaves to soups or batter them and deep fry. The leaf tops are a good source of vitamin B12 for vegans. Do not over use.

Dandelion (taraxacum officinale). Use as a spinach vegetable, and in salads, and torn into sandwiches with salt and pepper. If you grow dandelions for food, remove the flower heads. To blanch and lessen the bitterness, cover with a plant pot and straw. Perfect for early salads. A powerful blood cleanser and spring tonic.

STELLARIA MEDIA

TARAXACUM OFFICINALE

SPRING
fat hen to salad burnet

Fat Hen and *Good King Henry* (*chenopodium album/ bonus-henricus*). Spinach vegetables, eaten for over 2000 years, use in soups and stews.

Hawthorn (*crataegus monogyna*). Also known as 'bread and cheese', add the young shoots to salads. A nice nutty flavour.

Hop (*humulus lupulus*). Steam the young leaf shoots.

Nettle (*stinging*) (*urtica dioica*). Traditionally the young nettle tops were used in the spring for nettle soup, nettle beer, and nettle pudding. A powerful tonic.

Orache (*common*) (*atriplex patula*). Excellent flavour. Boil the leaves as a vegetable.

Rampion (*campanula rapunculus*). Formerly grown in kitchen gardens for its spinach-type leaves and its roots. The shoots can be eaten in the spring like asparagus. Well worth growing in your garden. Do not allow the plant to flower.

Salad Burnet (*sanguisorba minor*). The leaves have a sharp flavour, and are a great addition to salads. An attractive plant to grow in the garden.

CHENOPODIUM ALBUM

SANGUISORBA MINOR

SPRING
sea-beet to wood sorrel

Seabeet or *Sea Spinach* (*beta vulgaris*). The wild plant fom which our cultivated spinach comes.

Sorrel (*common*) (*rumex acetosa*). One of the best-known spinach vegetables. Easy to find as it grows everywhere. Add to almost anything. It is also a blood cleanser and beneficial to the whole system.

Tansy (*tanacetum vulgare*). Traditionally the young leaves were used at Easter in puddings, cakes and in egg dishes. They are very bitter, so use sparingly.

Yellow Rocket (*or winter cress*) (*barbarea vulgaris*). The leaves start to grow in the Autumn and continue throughout the winter and the spring. Cook them or eat in salad. If you grow this in your garden, nip out the flower buds of most (eat them in salad); this will keep a good supply of fresh green leaves. A general tonic.

Wood Sorrel (*oxalis acetosella*). A salad vegetable in the 14th century, and an attractive plant to grow in shaded areas of the garden. The leaves may be added to salads and soups. A sharp but delicate flavour, not to be over-used.

OXALIS ACETOSELLA

SPRING RECIPES

Spinach-type greens

Combining different spring leaves brings a variety of tastes and textures. Like all greens, a huge pile of leaves is reduced to a small heap when cooked, so pick plenty.

Wash the leaves, and cook them gently without any more water in an saucepan with a lid. This will take about five minutes. Drain off the liquid, saving it for soups by pressing the leaves with the back of a wooden spoon. Season with salt and pepper, and add a knob of butter. Cover and leave to stand for a few minutes before serving.

Anything is possible; some favourites:

- Finely chop and add to omelettes or quiches.
- Add fried onions and mushrooms, slices of garlic and diced cheese. Then return to the heat briefly until the cheese melts.
- Add fried onions, hazelnuts or peanut butter, tomatoes and soya sauce. Serve with rice.
- Mix the chopped cooked spinach with cottage cheese, two eggs and some grated cheese. Pour into a dish lined with pastry. Bake in a medium oven for half an hour.

RUMEX ACETOSA

SPRING RECIPES

SPRING RECIPES
herb pudding & nettle soup

Herb Pudding

Traditionally made in the spring: In a muslin bag, lay alternate layers of wild greens (bistort, sorrel and nettle tops are best) and a cereal (medium oatmeal or barley are traditional, but I like rice). Add a little salt and pepper between the layers. Tie the whole thing up and boil for half an hour until the grain has swelled, the leaves have shrunk and the flavours have mingled. Turn out onto a dish of beaten eggs, which instantly cook in the heat, or onto a bed of chopped hard boiled eggs.

Nettle Soup

A basic recipe which can be adapted to include other wild greens: Sweat some chopped onions, garlic and potato slices in butter. Add this to a vegetable stock, and add a bowlful of washed nettle tops. Bring to the boil and cover. Simmer until cooked (about fifteen minutes). If possible, liquidize the soup, if not, use a whisk to break it up. Add salt, pepper, nutmeg and cream. Serve with a swirl of cream on the top.

URTICA DIOICA

SPRING RECIPES
batter, tansy pancakes, stems & young shoots

Basic Batter Recipe

Beat together one egg and three tablespoons each of milk, water and plain flour. Gradually add a little more water until it is smooth and creamy. Add a little salt, and leave to stand for at least half an hour. Rebeat just before you use it. Wash leaves, flowers, slices of mushroom or fruit, dust with flour, dip in batter and then straight into a saucepan of very hot oil. Turn almost immediately. They are ready in a minute. Drain and serve either as part of a savoury dish or serve dipped into cream, sugar, or honey.

Tansy Pancakes

To the basic batter recipe add orange rind, chopped fresh tansy leaves and some cream and sherry. In a very hot frying pan add some oil and pour in some of the pancake mixture. As soon as the pancake loosens, turn and cook the other side. Serve with squeezed oranges, sugar, cream or yoghurt.

Stems and Young Shoots

Strip off the leaves, tie in bundles, steam quickly and serve with butter and black pepper.

SUMMER
wild herbs & flowers

The summer months are the traditional time to gather wild herbs. They are useful additions to salads and summer pies and are also worth gathering, hanging up to dry and storing for the winter months, when they can be lavishly added to soups and stews. They have less flavour than cultivated herbs so you need more of them. They are very hardy and can easily be grown along the hedgerows of your garden for a wealth of different flavours to add to your cooking.

Flowers are also a source of food at this time of year. They can be added to salads, and make stunning garnishes. Many of the mushrooms, nuts and fruits discussed in the Autumn section of this book begin to appear in the late summer.

Listed below and overleaf are some of the more common and delicious wild herbs:

Cleavers (*galium aparine*). A bitter leaf, but the seeds may be roasted in a pan for an excellent coffee substitute.

Hairy Bittercress (*cardamine hirsuta*). Use the leaves and flowers from the middle of the plant, adding to salads. A sharp spicey flavour not unlike watercress.

SUMMER

CARDAMINE HIRSUTA

MELISSA OFFICINALIS

MYRRHIS ODORATA

SUMMER HERBS

Hedge Garlic (*alliaria petiolata*). Mild flavoured oniony garlic leaf. Pick before the plant flowers.

Lemon Balm (*melissa officinalis*). Pleasant lemon taste. Use in salads, puddings and summer drinks.

Marjoram (*origanum vulgare*). Use in tomato dishes, pasta recipes, eggs, salads and in soups.

Sweet Cicely or Myrrh (*myrrhis odorata*). Chop the leaves into omlettes and salad dressings. Cook the leaves with tart fruits such as gooseberries or rhubarb to reduce the acidity and bring sweetness to the fruit.

Ramsons or *Wild Garlic* (*allium ursinium*). Use the young leaves before the flowers have died. Strong garlic flavour which can be added to soups, omelettes, bread, butter, salads and eaten fresh in sandwiches.

Thyme (wild) (*thymus serpyllum*). Add to soups, stews, salads, egg and tomato dishes.

Wild Fennel (*foeniculum vulgare*). Add leaves and stalks to salads, egg and fish dishes. Use the leaves fresh in sandwiches. Add the seeds to bread. Avoid the bulb.

ALLIARIA PETIOLATA

FOENICULUM VULGARE

SUMMER FLOWERS
broom to elderflower

Flowers are used as a garnish, sprinkled into salad or fruit salad. Use them for a spark of unusual colour or flavour. They can also be dipped in batter and deep fried, made into summer drinks, and candied. Only pick wild flowers if there are alot of them. Never overpick. Growing them yourself is best, as they need to be used fresh and you are then not robbing from the wild.

Broom (*sarothamnus scoparius*). Flowers March to June. Add the buds to salads, or toss into stir-fry vegetables at the last minute.

Borage (*borago officinalis*). Flowers mid-summer. Add the bright blue flowers to salads, fruits salads or fruit cups. Good candied.

Cowslips (*primula veris*). Flowers mid to late spring. Add to salads, also can be candied.

Camomile (*anthemis nobilis*). Flowers mid-summer to autumn. A refreshing, calming and soothing tea.

Elder (*sambucus nigra*). Flowers late spring. Herbal tea, cordial, champagne, wine. The whole flower head is good battered and deep fried.

SAROTHAMNUS SCOPARIUS

SUMMER FLOWERS
hawthorn to wild rose

Hawthorn (*crataegus monogyna*). Flowers May to June. Sprinkle into salads, fruit salads and fruit cups. Used for making wine, liqueur, and a refreshing herbal tea.

Lime (*tilia vulgaris*). Flowers mid-summer. For Herbal tea.

Marigold (*calendula officinalis*). Flowers in August. Add the petals to salads and soups. In the past the dried petals were added to winter soups. A good herbal tea.

Nasturtium (*tropaeolum majus*). Flowers midsummer to autumn. Add the leaves and flower buds to salads. Batter the whole flower and deep fry. A hot, spicy, cress-like flavour and a stunning garnish.

Pansy (*viola wittrockiana*) & *Primrose* (*primula vulgaris*). Use in salads and as a garnish. Both can be candied.

Red Clover (*trifolium pratense*). Flowers May to September. Use in salads and battered.

Violet (*sweet*) (*violata ordorata*). Flowers early spring. Good in salads, fruits salads, and to flavour rice dishes and ground rice puddings.

Wild Rose (*dog rose*) (*rosa canina*). For salads, rose petal jam, wine, and can be candied.

ROSA CANINA

TILIA VULGARIS

27

SUMMER RECIPES
herbs in butters, flans, vinegars & oils

Herbs in Cooking

Add to soups, stocks and casseroles at the beginning of cooking, and to cooked vegetables and sauces ten minutes before the end of cooking. Use herbs in breadmaking, nut roasts, stuffings, vegetable flans, quiches and omelettes.

Herb Butters

Chop some herbs, add some lemon juice, salt and black pepper. Beat into the butter until it is a smooth paste.

Herb Flan

Combine chopped herbs, onions and garlic with plenty of cottage cheese and one or two beaten eggs. Add black pepper, pour into a pie dish lined with pastry. Sprinkle with grated cheese and bake in a medium oven for about 40 minutes. Perfect with salad.

Herbal Vinegar and Herbal Oils

For salad dessings and marinades. Loosely fill a clean wide-necked jar with freshly picked herbs. Pour in warmed wine vinegar or olive oil to fill the jar. Place in a sunny window and shake daily for two weeks. Strain off the herbs and rebottle. For salad dressings and marinades.

TROPAEOLUM MAJUS

SUMMER RECIPES

SUMMER RECIPES
floral vinegars, rose petal jelly & candied flowers

Floral Vinegars

Make in the same way as herbal vinegar, using any edible flower. Remove stalks and green or white bases from the petals. Use in fruit salads.

Rose Petal Jelly

Dissolve two cups of sugar in half a cup of water. Add one tablespoon each of orange juice and lemon juice, and two cups of well packed wild rose petals. Cook gently, stirring continuously for half an hour until the petals have melted. Cool, then pour into a jam jar and keep cold. Use with yoghurt, ice cream, pancakes and waffles.

Candied Flowers

Very relaxing to do. Remove the stalks and white bases from the petals. Beat an egg white until foamy. Dip each flower or petal into the egg white and then dip in sugar. Place on a sheet of greaseproof paper on a cooling rack. When full, cover with another sheet and leave in a very low oven with the door open until dry. Store in an airtight container. Use as cake and dessert decorations.

BORAGO OFFICINALIS

SUMMER RECIPES
summer teas, liqueurs & elderflower cordial

Summer Flower Teas

Pour boiling water onto some flowers or herbs. Cover and leave for ten minutes. Remove the leaves and flowers and add some honey or sugar. Cool. Can be served chilled with ice cubes and slices of lemon.

May Blossom Liqueur

Pack the blossoms into a wide-mouthed bottle. Sprinkle in two tablespoons of sugar. Fill the bottle with brandy and cork. Shake daily for three weeks. Filter out the blossom and rebottle. Try using other edible flowers, vodka or gin.

Elderflower Cordial

A firm family favourite. In a large bowl put ten elderflower heads, one and a half pounds of sugar, two chopped lemons and one ounce of tartaric acid. Pour on four pints of boiling water. Stir well. Cover with a tea towel and leave for twenty-four hours, stirring occasionally. Strain through muslin and pour into bottles. Can be used straight away or kept for a few weeks. Dilute with water. Elderflower Cordial can be stored for longer if the bottles are sterilised and corked.

CRATAEGUS MONOGYNA

SAMBUCUS NIGRA

SUMMER RECIPES
summer pudding & pickled walnuts

Many fruits, nuts and mushrooms (found in the Autumn section of this book) can first be found during August. The first pickings of wild fruit can be made into that classic old favourite:

Summer Pudding

Rinse a pudding basin with cold water and line it with bread, making sure there are no gaps. Cook two pounds of mixed wild fruit for a few minutes in two to three tablespoons of water and three tablespoons of sugar. Strain off a cupful of juice and pour the rest into the lined basin. Cover with bread, put a plate and a weight on the top and leave overnight. In the morning invert the pudding over a plate and pour over the remaining fruit juice. Serve with cream.

Pickled Walnuts

Pick the young green nuts in July. Prick them with a fork and leave them covered in a strong brine for a week, until they are black. Drain, wash them, and let them dry for two days. Pack them into jars and cover with hot pickling vinegar. Seal the jars and eat after one month.

JUGLANS REGIA

AUTUMN
edible hedgerow fruit

As we pass from high summer into autumn, the hedgerows are rich with the fruits of the season. Much of this can be eaten fresh in puddings, but it can also be preserved for the months ahead, as jams, jellies, syrups, wine and liqueurs.

Bilberry (*vaccinium myrtilis*). August and September. Eat raw or cook with sugar, lemon juice and peel. Use in pies, open tarts, on pancakes and for jam. Native Americans dried them for winter soups and stews.

Blackberry (*rubus fruticosus*). Everyone's favourite. Eat them raw with sugar and cream, or bake them into pies and crumbles. Mix them with stewed apple. Make jam, jelly, wine and vinegar.

Bullace (*prunus insititia*). October and November. The wild damson. Leave on the tree until the first frosts have reduced their acidity. Use for pies, jams and wines.

Cherry Plum (*prunus cerasifera*). September. For pies (use plenty of sugar), jams and liqueurs.

Crab Apple (*pyrus malus*). September to December. Jelly, wine, cider, verjuice. Can be mixed with other apples.

AUTUMN

VACCINIUM MYRTILIS

RUBUS FRUTICOSUS

AUTUMN FRUITS

Elderberry (*sambucus nigra*). September and October. Jam, jelly, cordial, wine, vinegar and chutney. Can be mixed with stewed apples and other fruit.

Hawthorn (*crateagus oxyacantha*). September to November. The haws can be made into wine, conserve, dried for fruit tea and for making haw brandy.

Juniper (*juniperus communis*). Add to other fruit for pies and jam. Can be dried and added to soup and stew in the winter. Can be made into juniper gin.

Nasturtium (*tropaeolum majus*). September. Add the seeds to salads or pickle them in vinegar to resemble capers.

Rosehip (*rosa canina*). August - November. Made into purée for pies in the 17th century, but completely clearing out the insides is very time consuming. Use to make rosehip syrup. Strain several times through muslin and boil with sugar. Also makes excellent wine.

Rowan (*sorbus aucuparia*). August to November. The berries make an excellent jelly. Add some chopped crab apples to ensure it sets.

Sloes (*blackthorn*) (*prunus spinosa*). October to November. Pick after the first frost. For jelly, wine and sloe gin.

SORBUS AUCUPARIA

JUNIPERUS COMMUNIS

HEDGEROW NUTS

Nuts are great for free protein which can be stored for the winter. Be sure to dry them properly and keep them in a basket somewhere dry.

Almond (*amygdalus communis*). Blanch to peel off the skin. Use in soups, stews and salads. Grind to a flour for cakes and biscuits. Use to thicken any sauce.

Hazel (*corylus avellana*). Late August to October. The green nuts may be eaten raw. Otherwise use them in cakes, biscuits or make them into nut butters and spreads. They can also be used for nut roasts and nut burgers.

Sweet Chestnut (*castanea sativa*). October and November. Slit the inner shell and roast by the fire or on a shovel over the fire, or in the oven. They may be boiled, skinned and made into purée, chestnut stuffing, burgers and soup.

Walnut (*juglans regia*). October to November. Use in savoury recipes such as stir-fry vegetables, tomato dishes with pasta, or salad dishes with rice. Also bake in cakes. Green walnuts may be pickled.

CORYLUS AVELLANA

CASTANEA SATIVA

41

MUSHROOMS & FUNGI

This is an extensive aspect of wild food cookery, but here I include just a few common varieties. Please use a good field guide and gather only what you are sure of.

The best way to pick a mushroom is to gently twist it at the base. Then check they are not grub-infested by cutting through the stem with a knife. Only pick the youngest mushrooms, on a dry day. Handle them gently, laying them in a basket if possible.

Eat mushrooms as soon as possible or dry them by threading them onto string and hanging them in a dry warm place until they are brittle. Store in airtight containers and use in winter soups and stews.

Cep (*xerocomus badius*). Traditionally known as the Penny Bun in this country. Easy to recognise, this brown bun-shaped mushroom has a white spongey underside instead of gills, gradually turning yellowish, and then olive green in old age.

Chantarelle (*cantarellus cibarius*). Yellowy orange and funnel shaped. Especially good with eggs. Unsuitable for drying.

XEROCOMUS BADIUS

CANTHARELLUS CIBARIUS

43

MUSHROOMS & FUNGI
field mushrooms, puffballs, parasols and inkcaps

Field & Horse Mushrooms (*agaricus campester & arvensis*).
These most familiar white mushrooms have pink gills
underneath, darkening to brown as they mature. They
can only be confused with two others: the Yellow
Stainer, which turns bright yellow when you slice it,
and the Blusher, which turns pink. Fry in butter or
olive oil and eat fresh on toast, or fry and stew in a
little milk. Use in pies, soup, sauces, with eggs and
with cream.

Common Puffball (*lycoperdon perlatum*). May be anything
from the size of a grapefruit to the size of a football.
Check the flesh is white and fresh. Cut into half inch
slices and fry. Great between slices of bread and all
other mushroom dishes.

Parasol (*macrolepiota procera*). Pick just as the cap begins to
open, as the caps can become dry. Good dipped in
batter and deep fried. Stems are too woody to eat.

Shaggy Inkcap (*coprinus comatus*). Only pick the ones which
are tightly closed as they go slimey quickly. Cook as
soon as possible. Good battered whole.

ACARICUS CAMPESTER

MACROLEPIOTA PROCERA

ROOTS

Roots are dug with a spade from August onwards and are good until the hard frosts. Some will overwinter.

Alexanders (*smyrnium olusatrum*). Eaten like parsnips.

Burdock (*arctium minus*). May be roasted whole, or sliced thinly in stir fries. Dandelion & burdock beer.

Dandelion (*taraxacum officinale*). Sliced into stir fries, salads, stews etc. For an excellent healthy coffee, wash and dry the roots, spread onto a baking tray and bake in the oven until brown and brittle, then grind.

Horseradish (*armoracia rusticana*). Horseradish sauce.

Jerusalem Artichoke. Worth growing along a hedgerow. A good standby in autumn and winter. Good with cheese sauce poured over the boiled bulbs.

Lovage (*ligusticum scoticum*). Aromatic flavoured root vegetable, formerly eaten in the Scottish Highlands.

Rampion (*campanula rapunculus*). Boil the roots and serve with a sauce. Slice the young roots in winter salad. Earth the roots up in the summer to blanch them. Nip out the flower buds. Rare in the wild.

TARAXACUM OFFICINALE

AUTUMN RECIPES
fruit jellies and jams

Traditionally autumn fruits were preserved for winter use by bottling, making syrups, jams, jellies, cheeses, conserves and chutneys. They also make excellent wines and liqueurs. Here I include just a few of my favourites:

Crab Apple Jelly

Rough chop six pounds of crab apples and boil in water with slices of ginger root and a sliced lemon. Pour the pulp in a jelly bag to drip overnight (do not squeeze!). Return the liquid to the pan and add a pound of sugar to each pint of juice. Rapid boil for half an hour until it begins to set when tested on a plate. Cool and pour into clean warmed jars.

Blackberry and Apple Jelly is made by the same method, using equal amounts of cooking apples and blackberries.

Elderberry and Apple Jam

Quick and easy and a firm favourite. Make a pulp by boiling two pounds of rough chopped apples in some water, and pass through a sieve to remove seeds, core and skin. Do the same with two pounds of elderberries (just a little water needed). Combine the two pulps, adding four pounds of sugar and boil for about ten minutes until it thickens. Makes seven jars of jam.

MALUS SYLVESTRIS

AUTUMN
RECIPES

AUTUMN RECIPES
sloe gin & elderberry chutney

Sloe Gin

Prick one and a quarter pints of sloes and put them into a wide-necked jar. Sprinkle in two ounces of sugar and pour in a bottle of gin or vodka. Cork and shake daily for three months. Strain off the fruit and filter back into bottles. Best left for a year if you can resist the temptation. The gin soaked sloes can be mixed with melted chocolate for a special treat.

Many other fruit liqueurs can be made in the same way using damsons, bullace, crap apples and so on. Haw brandy is a traditional liqueur made by the same method with hawthorn berries and brandy.

Elderberry Chutney

Stalk and wash two pounds of elderberries. Put them in a pan and bruise them with a wooden spoon. Add a large chopped onion, a pint of vinegar and two tablespoon of sugar. Next add one teaspoon each of salt, ground ginger and mustard seeds, and half a teaspoon each of cayenne pepper and mixed spice. Bring to the boil and simmer until it becomes thick. Then put into warmed jars when cool.

PRUNUS SPINOSA

MUSHROOM RECIPES

Mushrooms in Milk

(Serves two). Fry a pound of mushrooms in a little butter, together with some finely chopped onions. Add about three quarters of a pint of milk and bring slowly to the boil, stirring constantly. Add a sprig of thyme, salt and pepper, and simmer gently for three quarters of an hour. Thicken with a little cornflour mixed with cold water. Pour over toast, potatoes, pasta or boiled root vegetables.

Mushroom Soup

Simply add extra water to the above recipe.

Mushroom Fritters

Use the basic batter recipe on page 18. Wash the mushrooms, either leaving whole if unopened, or slice. Coat lightly in flour, dip in the batter and deep fry until golden brown. Wonderfully succulent.

Mushroom and Potato Cakes

Mix together cooked mashed potatoes, some milk, butter, grated cheese and diced fresh mushrooms. Knead in enough flour to bind the mixture together. Form into cakes on a floured board and fry until golden brown. Serve with salad.

NUT RECIPES

Roasted Nuts

Spread on an oiled tray and bake in the oven at 190°C for ten minutes. Or gently cook in a frying pan in very little oil.

Hazelnut Butter or Chocolate Hazelnut Spread

Grind nuts into a powder and blend with soft butter. To make the spread just beat in some cocoa powder!

Nut Roast

Nut roast can be made using a variety of ingredients. Here is a favourite: Lightly fry a diced onion and two finely diced courgettes. Add 4oz chopped hazelnuts, a tablespoon of cumin seeds, half a tablespoon of sesame seeds, half a teaspoon of turmeric and quarter of a teaspoon of ginger. Pour in 4oz tomato puree, 4oz rolled oats (or rice, or bread-crumbs), 2oz ground nuts, 2oz coconut, half a teaspoon of mixed herbs and some salt and pepper. Press into an oiled dish and bake at 180°C for thirty-five minutes.

Walnut Balls

Combine ground walnuts, breadcrumbs, grated cheese, grated onion, a diced red pepper, chopped parsley, season-ing, and a beaten egg. Form into balls, then bake or fry.

ROOT RECIPES

Dandelion and Burdock Beer

Scrub two large dandelion roots and two large burdock roots. Chop them into a pan with four pints of water. Boil for half an hour. In another pan, gently dissolve one pound of sugar in four pints of water with two tablespoons of black treacle and the juice of a lemon. Strain off the roots, mix the two liquids together and leave to go tepid. Then add an ounce of yeast mixed to a paste in warm water. Leave to ferment in a covered bucket for three to four days, then bottle. Ready to drink after one week.

Horseradish Sauce

Cut off the skin and grate the white root. Do this outside as the fumes are very strong. Combine the freshly grated horseradish with yoghurt or double cream, adding some seasoning and a little sugar, mustard powder and wine vinegar to taste. Great with cheese on toast!

Root Salad

Slice the roots to the size of matchsticks. Steam or boil in water. Drain, cool and combine with mayonnaise or another sauce.

ARMORACIA RUSTICANA

WINTER

Winter is the time to use all the things you have saved from the year's foraging, adding dried herbs, mushrooms, nuts and berries to soups and stews, and preserved fruits to puddings.

There are a few plants which can be found in the winter, all of which have been used since ancient times, and are worth encouraging into your garden: Chickweed (*stellaria media*), Hairy Bittercress (*cardamine hirsuta*), Sow Thistle (*sonchus oleraceus*), and Common Wintercress (also known as Yellow Rocket) (*barbarea vulgaris*).

Combine what leaves you can find with a chopped orange, nuts, olive oil, salt, pepper and a little wine vinegar for a refreshing winter salad.

Dandelion leaves may be forced under plant pots which are covered with straw. If the winter is mild they are available throughout.

The roots and leaves of Rampion (*campanula rapunculus*) can be used in the winter, and Salsify (*tragopogon porrifolius*) is another old traditional vegetable formerly grown for its roots, which can be baked, boiled and served with a white, herb or cheese sauce, and made into a creamy soup.

BARBAREA VULGARIS

WINTER

NOTES